They Are Not Going To Save Us

Essays, Poems, Lyrics, Notes, Et Cetera

Wambui Bahati

They Are Not Going To Save Us

Library of Congress Control Number: 2009929912

ISBN 978-09822398-3-4

Cover Design by JLW World Press

●JLW●World●Press●

Published by JLW World Press
New York, NY / Greensboro, NC
888-224-2267

Dedicated to

Marie and Julie

Introduction:
A Note from the Author

Every since I can remember I've love being creative. I love anything that involves the imagination. I love anything that involves creating something out of nothing—or taking something and turning it into something else even more spectacular.

I fell in love with theater and performing at a very young age, but I was also in love with writing and crafts and sewing and making things with Popsicle sticks, or aluminum foil, or rhinestones, or rocks and leaves. In this book I share some of my ideas, my thoughts and my perspective on various topics in a variety of ways.

I had fun putting this book together. The title of this book, *They Are Not Going to Save Us* is the lead essay in this book. However, the title is also appropriate because I know it has been the arts, creativity and my imagination that has 'saved' me and allowed me to remain standing in the face of many difficult challenges.

Knowing that the answers are within me—that all of us have been born with an inmate wisdom and intelligence that most of us have forgotten how to tap into has given me the strength to take full responsibility for my life. Through many of the writings in this book I encourage the reader to be quiet, go within, and understand that you are already victorious.

The solutions to our challenges will not come from the 'powers that be' or the powerful people or systems outside of us. The answers will come from the power within us. We must find and create our own realities and not allow anything outside of us to dictate who we are and limit what we can do.

I create with the understanding that creativity and my imagination takes me away from the 3-D world. While I am away, ideas, answers, and solutions as to what I must do to resolve any 'seemingly' unpleasant issues will come to me effortlessly.

As I sit here today, I understand that I could either focus on financial challenges—or, I could create.

Enjoy!

Peace,
Wambui

Table of Contents

They Are Not Going To Save Us

I am convinced there are some things that *they* do not want YOU to know about YOU. If you knew who you <u>really</u> are and what you are capable of, you would be healthier and happier — and richer. Most of us, however, have adopted the idea that so-called experts know what is best for us. Therefore, we entrust our power, and our money, to the government, health care systems, educational systems, insurance companies, and various other agencies set up to protect us. *They*, however, are not going to save us.

Where Is the Cure?

Look around at what is happening in our world and our communities. How many years have we been marching, running, and cycling for "the cure?" Are we healthier? Why are there new diseases each year?

Why are there more medications for these diseases, as well as the same old diseases year after year? The health statistics are more disturbing each year.

• According to the Mental Health Association, 1 in 5 adults suffers from a diagnosable mental disorder in a given year.

• In the U.S., 21.9 million adults and 8.9 million children under 18 have been diagnosed with asthma (Allergy & Asthma Network Mothers of Asthmatics - AANMA).

• Nearly 1 in 3 adults has high blood pressure (The American Heart Association).

•More than 1,500 people die of cancer each day (American Cancer Society).

• There has been a 500 percent increase in the number of prescriptions written for ADHD since 1991 (Education-world.com).

Controlled

We are being poisoned and suppressed, mentally and spiritually, by the chemicals in our food and water, the polluted air we breathe, and by the high levels of electromagnetic waves in our environment. Can it be that the well-educated men and women in positions of power in this country and in the world cannot figure out what needs to happen to turn these health statistics around? Could it be about money, power and control? Yes, they are taking your money, your power, and you are being controlled. *They* are not going to save us.

The Good News

Understanding that no one is coming to save us is <u>good news</u>. This means we can stop sitting around waiting on a promise and can take charge of our own lives — and our own health. Yes, we can do this. Our bodies are miraculous. Our spirits are divine.

We can start by simply knowing what it is we are putting into and on our bodies. A simple rule that I follow is if I cannot pronounce it, I do not eat it.

Whole Entities

If you are eating and drinking items that you would not feel comfortable putting *on* your skin, then do not put them *into* your body. The reverse is also true, if you are using products on the outside of your body that you would not feel comfortable putting into your mouth and inside your body, then perhaps you should consider using different products.

We should start looking at our bodies as whole entities and know that whether the chemicals are inside or outside, they have the ability to affect us -or not affect us — in one way or another. Understand that the food you eat does affect you physically, mentally and spiritually. Understand that your environment does affect you physically, mentally and spiritually.

Something Simple

You may be allergic to some food or some item in your environment that you are not even aware of. For instance, there have been great healing successes for people when they simply removed white bread and other wheat products from their diet. Many people find that they feel better when they do not eat dairy products.

I am not saying that this is the case for everybody. What I am saying is, sometimes the culprit that is making us feel ill can be something simple. I recently read that a man received great relief from a constant, nagging back problem by simply moving his bed away from a wall that electrical current ran through. There is also data available that proves the healing power of pure water.

Check out your environment for toxins — this includes toxic people, too. We can learn to love some people from afar.

A Spiritual Being

Understand that you are a spiritual being. What does this mean? It means we are in this world, but we are not of this world. Your body is your 3-D earthly container. Your body is not who you are. You see; you have always been and will forever be. You are pure God energy. You are a wonderful, beautiful, vibrating spirit.

You are of and from a greater source and will eventually return to that source. There is nothing that is true of God (or whatever you call the Greatest Entity) that is not true of ourselves. It means there is no one greater than you are, more powerful than you are, or wiser than you.

However, we have been convinced otherwise. For you to know these things would mean that you could no longer be controlled. It would mean that the ad agencies and the media's strategies of selling you on the idea that you need more and more things to be happy would not work.

Five Senses

At an early age, we are taught about our five senses. However, we are led to believe that if we cannot see something, hear it, touch it, taste it or smell it, it does not exist. This is not true. We do not see or smell the electromagnetic waves that make wireless phones possible. We cannot see, touch or smell radio and TV signals or see sound waves. Yet, they exist. Wow, what marvelous wonders must exist in us, around us, and through us that we are not able to experience with our five senses.

Good Vibrations

We are also taught about the many systems in our bodies, including the digestive system, the respiratory system, the nervous system and skeletal system. Rarely is there mention of our energy system. Although we cannot see our subtle energy fields, this vital force allows us access to greater wisdom, intuition and perfect health. So many times, when we are looking for the answers to our physical and mental challenges, we do not check our energy system to make sure it is balanced as well. We are vibrations. We are electric!

Look Inside

Most of us were never taught how to tap in to, or gain access to, our inner wisdom and our inner power. 'Knowledge of self' is not in the public school curriculum. We must stop looking outside ourselves and looking to everyone else to give us the answer and the cure. Many health care providers are dedicated, caring people. They can treat our symptoms and make us feel better. However, we must, and can, take responsibility for our own health and healing. Remember, *they* are not going to save us.

Television Fast

Several years ago, I threw my TV out. Well, I didn't literally throw it out. However, I did cancel cable and removed the television from the main areas of my home. That means no access to TV in the living room, dining area, or kitchen. I live in New York City in a tiny condominium. Therefore, when I say I removed the TV from my living room, dining area and kitchen, I'm talking only about one small TV.

For the first week or so, my daughter and I sat on the sofa and watched the space where the TV used to be. Then we got the idea that we could talk to each other while watching the space where the TV used to be. I'm not sure how it happened, but one day we sat on the sofa and started looking at each other (instead of at the space where the TV used to be) while we talked.

Even now, when friends or relatives come over to visit, after the initial greetings, someone always looks at the space where the TV use to be, gasps, and asks, "What happened to your TV?" My mother wondered if I was having financial difficulties that forced me to sell the TV.

I try to explain that I just did not want TV anymore. I have a reputation for being someone who goes against the norm, so most people see it as "just one of her things" or "a phase" that I will grow out of eventually. In the end, we talk to one another as we watch the space where the TV used to be. (I'm looking for a plant to put in that space.)

I do have a TV in my bedroom, which I use only for watching DVDs and videos. I have come to love living without TV. There is calmness in my home. There is an "I'm on vacation" feel. I feel more peaceful. I get a lot more done each day. I recently rediscovered my joy in writing. I sew. I read. I make stuff and call it art.

Eating a meal at home without TV felt lonely at first. I had come to think of TV as what you did when you ate. I had convinced myself that if I were eating while I was watching TV, then I was not just wasting time watching TV. Even if I was not watching it, I felt comfortable hearing TV sounds in the background. I grew up in one of those households where the TV was always on. During holiday meals, the TV was loud. However, the idea of turning the TV volume down never occurred to any of us, so we just talked louder.

Eating without TV has become a wonderful and healthy experience for me. I find that I eat less and am more concerned about what I'm eating. Many times, with TV, I would not even remember eating, but the food would be gone. It was like when you drive somewhere in your car and realize when you arrive that you have no recollection of any of the intersections, buildings and parks you know you passed to get there. I take time to enjoy my food now.

I did not watch much TV before. I watched an average of two — no three — maybe four hours a day — I think. That's the trouble with TV. The hours creep by unnoticed. One becomes hypnotized. I was becoming addicted to TV court shows. I was intrigued by the predicaments some people get themselves into. Often I would think to myself, "There, but for the grace of god, go I". I did learn from those shows to get every money transaction in writing — especially from your relatives.

I learned many years ago not to watch the news. As a person who suffered from depression for many years, I learned that watching the news did not agree with me — especially just before going to bed. Those news stories stay with you in your subconscious. Let's face it: Except for a warm and fuzzy human-interest story now and then, the news is not good. The old saying, "No news is good news" is true.

Once people find out I no longer have TV, they are eager to report the news to me and tell me what I missed on all of their favorite TV shows. "You didn't see it?" "You didn't hear about the little boy that found an alligator in his room?" I feel that if there is something I need to know, I'll find out somehow.

I do not know what the security alert color is now, and that suits me just fine. I have prepared my family and myself the best I can for an emergency. I figure if I ever see people running en masse in a certain direction, I will just join in and run, too. Meanwhile, I don't worry about it daily. I do check certain sites online for news about health products and changes in any laws that might affect me.

For a wonderful, healthy and pleasurable experience, I challenge you and your family to take a TV fast. TV addiction is real, and many people have difficulty breaking the TV habit. Your eyes, your brain, your ears, and your whole body will thank you. Take back your mind and your life. Deprogram!

Sometimes you just need to sit down and shut up.

What I Did the Last Time I Spent the Night in the Atlanta Airport

Recently I spent the night in the Atlanta airport. I've done this before. Atlanta's Hartsfield-Jackson Airport, a major connecting hub, is considered one of the world's busiest passenger airports. Therefore, when bad weather hits Atlanta, flights are grounded and hundreds of people end up stuck at the airport.

The plane I was to take from Wichita to Atlanta (at 11:30 a.m.) was delayed seven hours because of bad weather in Atlanta. By the time I got to Atlanta, there was bad weather in New York City, my final destination. Therefore, no planes were leaving for New York City that evening.

When it was finally my turn to ask the airline customer service agent how I would get home, I was told I had been booked on a flight that would leave the next morning at 6:45 a.m. for New York City. I was offered a discount coupon for a local hotel. I asked if I could get my checked bag back. I was told I could not.

I figured since I was going to have to spend the night in my clothes and without my toiletries anyway, why go to a hotel? It was about 9:30 p.m. I scouted the airport for what seemed like a reasonably comfortable chair. I figured out a way to keep my tote bag and computer bag straps wrapped around me while using both bags as a pillow.

After I closed my eyes, every ten minutes I heard a recorded announcement. I timed it. Every ten minutes a recorded voice would say, "The Homeland Security code is orange. We are on orange alert." Then the recording would say something about being cautious about people and packages around you.

Now, I don't watch television, especially late night news, because I don't want to hear about negative and disturbing events that I cannot control. I had discovered this practice of avoiding hearing about negative events when I was recovering from many years of depression. Hearing that we were on orange alert and hearing that I had to be more cautious about people and packages around me was not what I wanted to hear as I tried to fall asleep that evening. Listening to podcasts and tunes on my iPod helped for a while, but soon the battery power was too low.

I'm sure that someone decided to play the orange alert tape every ten minutes out of genuine concern for our safety. However, hearing it repeatedly was not serving me well at this particular time.

So I thought to myself, how can I make this work for me?

I decided to play a game. Whenever I heard the announcer say "orange", I would associate the color with something that I could relate to in a more pleasing and empowering way.

Therefore, I would substitute the word "love" for the word "orange". However corny this may sound, it worked for me. All through the night, "we were on 'love' alert." The mind is a powerful tool, and you can fool the psyche into believing anything you want it to believe. I decided that orange means love. Yes, we were on the security "love" level.

I figured that's really the most important thing we can do when we hear orange alert. We need to love. Love ourselves. Love our neighbors. And yes, love those who might want to harm us. I don't love what they do. However, I have learned that when I'm consumed with hate and fear I destroy myself—I give away my power—and I'm not going to do that anymore. When I hear the announcement about an orange alert, I think of love. I am alert, and I love. Orange is love.

I had a lot of time on my hands that evening. Except for Chick-fil-a, all the other food places, bookstores and magazine concessions were closed. Therefore, I gave new meaning to all of the colors in the Homeland Security Advisory System. I gave each color a word that meant something special to me.

For instance, red is faith. I figured that if we ever get to red, which is the highest and most severe security threat, we are going to need faith. We are going to have to remember everything we've ever been taught about belief in a higher power and belief in ourselves. We are going to have to remember everything we've ever been taught about our own strength and the power within us. From everything I've read, no one is really sure what will happen if that day ever comes. That is why faith is so important.

Red means go deep inside and remember that you're not alone in this universe. Red means remember that you are loved. Remember that we are in this world, but not of it. Red means courage. Red means knowing that whatever happens, each of us has the ability to overcome it and to rise above. Level red to me is the level of faith.

That night in Atlanta, at about two o'clock in the morning, I went back down the scale, and I started with green. To me, green represents peace. Green represents new beginnings—the greatest joy. Green is happiness and an ideal state of being. At level green, we all understand that we are all one from one divine source.

The next level is blue. Blue is the color of the never-ending sky and the vast ocean. Blue is possibilities. Blue is amazing. Blue represents adventure and potential. Blue represents the everyday challenges that force us to grow and to learn lessons whether we are ready to learn them or not. Blue is travel and a new idea. Level blue is the level of possibilities.

Yellow is radiant energy. I think of the sun. Yellow is innovative. Yellow is "yes, I can." Yellow is divine health and divine wealth. Yellow is laughter and smiles that can't be hidden.

And that brings us back to orange—love—and red—faith . . . I finally felt secure with the Homeland Security color-coded advisory system.

And that is what I did the last time I spent the night in the Atlanta airport. What did you do?

Maybelle's After-Hours Disco Bar and Grill

I'm talkin' 'bout Maybelle's after-hours disco
bar and grill.
The ribs are succulent.
The pig feet are divine.
With any order you get your choice of free beer
or wine.

Just go straight down Washington Street,
Cross over Martin Luther King,
Right behind Tabernacle Church
Maybelle's can be seen.

Now down at Maybelle's they got their own
fashion rules.
Listen up girls and I'll tell you what to do.

Now the ladies mostly sport a fashion wig or at
least some type of weave.
The women wear tight-fitting skirts that stop
well above the knee.
Get yourself some spiked high heels—or some
platforms will do.
Lord, the men at Maybelle's will be all over you.

Now guys, at Maybelle's, wearing a suit is what
you want to do.
But please don't show up at Maybelle's wearing
brown, black or blue.
Yellow, purple and red are some colors that the
men sport around.
Maybelle's men may not have all their teeth but
they are the hottest dressers and best lovers in
town.

I'm talkin' 'bout Maybelle's after-hours disco
bar and grill
The ribs are succulent.
The pig feet are divine.
With any order you get your choice of free beer
or wine.

Just go straight down Washington Street,
Cross over Martin Luther King,
Right behind Tabernacle Church
Maybelle's can be seen.

It is right next to Lee Roy's Check Cash and
Pawn and Loan.
Right across the street from where you pay to
get your phone back on.

Now make sure you bring a handkerchief or
napkin up in there.
You gon' need it when you start to sweat cause
Maybelle's ain't got no air.

Girls, make sure your sugar daddy has cashed
his pay.
Cause Maybelle don't take no credit cards and
no checks—no way.

At least once a month if you are at Maybelle's
chillin',
You gon' have to go down to the courthouse to
testify about a killin'.

The chalk outlines all over the floor add a flare
to Maybelle's design.
But other than a few shootins' and stabbins'
Maybelle's don't have no crime.

I'm talkin' 'bout Maybelle's after-hours disco
bar and grill
The ribs are succulent.
The pig feet are divine.
With any order you get your choice of free beer
or wine.

Just go straight down Washington Street,
Cross over Martin Luther King,
Right behind Tabernacle Church
Maybelle's can be seen.

Whatever you are into,
You can get into at Maybelle's.
Whatever you groove to,
You can groove to it at Maybelle's.

The DJ at Maybelle's spins the funkiest blues.
That music will have you dancin' right out of
your shoes.

No heavy drugs are allowed in the spot
But you can smoke your cigarettes and maybe
a little pot.

I'm talkin' 'bout Maybelle's after-hours disco
bar and grill
The ribs are succulent.
The pig feet are divine.
With any order you get your choice of free beer
or wine.

Just go straight down Washington Street,
Cross over Martin Luther King,
Right behind Tabernacle Church
Maybelle's can be seen.

Watching You

Somebody is always watching you
Somebody always knows
Don't believe nobody sees what you do
Because every eye ain't closed

Everybody's not counting sheep
Every shut eye is not sleep
There is always somebody watching you and
you and you and you and you . . .

Nowhere to run
Nowhere to hide

Pop the champagne
Enjoy the ride

They know your numbers

They know your name

They scan your body

Before you get on a plane

Nowhere to run

Nowhere to hide

Pop the champagne

Enjoy the ride

O o o o oh sa a ay can you see . . . ?

I Don't Need to Need Somebody

I cannot hide my feelings so I just let them show.

I try to push you out of my mind but I cannot let you go.

I tell myself I would be better off if I just lived without you.

And even as I'm saying those words I know I'm a liar too.

Sometimes I feel so low and sad—many days I've cried.

I'll never fulfill the dream I had of being your beautiful bride.

I thought I'd be all right when you said that we were through,

I guess I'm not as strong as I thought because I
still want you.

I don't need to need somebody,
I am my own best friend.
If only I could believe these words
I could begin my life again.
I'm strong, I'm smart—I know I'll carry on,
But it's really hard to keep the faith now that
you are gone.

Secretly I call you in the middle of the night.
Don't tell a soul—no one must know, they
would say that I'm not right.

No one must know that without you my life is
so tough.
Long ago I convinced them all I was made of
stronger stuff.

I am still in shock from watching you walk out
my front door.
The tears fell from my eyes and my limp body
hit the floor.

I don't want my friends to know that I'm acting like a fool.
I can't be acting crazy when they know me as calm and cool.

I don't need to need somebody,
I am my own best friend.
If only I could believe these words
I could begin my life again.
I'm strong, I'm smart—I know I'll carry on,
But it's really hard to keep the faith now that you are gone.

Baby, make it easy—please; come on back home to me.
Every since you've been gone I can hardly eat or sleep—I don't want to be free.
I'm trying to be positive in the face of a negative blow.
I'm trying to be an independent woman, but it hurts to see you go.

Losing you took a toll on me—I'm spinning out of control.

I'm fighting back with all I have but there is damage to my soul.

Will you consider being my best platonic friend?
At least I might have a chance of seeing you every now and then.

I don't need to need somebody,
I am my own best friend.
If only I could believe these words
I could begin my life again.
I'm strong, I'm smart—I know I'll carry on,
But it's really hard to keep the faith now that you are gone.

I don't know what to do with myself,
I've been disturbed every since you left.

I'm doing all I can to keep from going insane,
My body and spirit ache with pain.

My hearts on fire, I have a desire
To hold you tighter—never let you go,
I love you so.

I don't need to need somebody,

I am my own best friend.

If only I could believe these words

I could begin my life again.

I'm strong, I'm smart—I know I'll carry on,

But it's really hard to keep the faith now that

you are gone.

NOTE: Do not take yourself or life too seriously. (*I know. Easier said than done.*) Life is a journey. We will travel on good roads and not-so-good roads; and have sunny days and stormy days.

When we are traveling in our car to see a friend or to a vacation spot and it starts to rain—or even snow, we may be disappointed. However, in the end, we accept it for what it is—bad weather.

We continue on through the storm, pull over to the side of the road, or turn around and go back home.

And, so it is with life's journey. Let's just see life's journey for what it is—good times and 'seemingly' bad times. It's that simple. How we deal with the journey depends on our perspective.

When you hit a stormy area, continue on through the storm if you can. However, do not try to fight bad weather. It is okay to pull over to the side of the road. Protect your loved ones and yourself. Do the best you can with what you have.

After you have done all you know to do, have a healthy snack and sing some songs with your family and friends while waiting for the storm to let up. The best ideas and solutions come when we are in a relaxed and a joyful state.

Do not let bad weather ruin your vacation or your life journey.

SELF: Got it. Thanks.

What Am I Going to Do?

Lord, Lord, Lord, what am I going to do?
If it ain't one thing, it's two.

I never thought I'd fall in love with you.

The day I marched down the aisle in my
wedding gown,
I told everyone I was finally settling down.
But I had one more oat to sew,
And I really didn't know
That there was a man like you.

Lord, Lord, Lord, what am I going to do?

Whenever it rains it pours,
It's hard to walk away from love like yours,
I told my new husband that I would never lie,

I'd always be with him until the day I die.

Now I'm seeing you on the side,

Another deceitful bride,

I have fallen in love with you.

Lord, Lord, Lord, what am I going to do?

If it ain't one thing, it's two.

Saturday Night Bath

I took a bath on Saturday night,
Just in time for Sunday.
If I do not sweat a lot,
I can make it last till Monday.

10 Tips for Relieving Depression

1. Eat life-giving foods.

If you eat devitalized and lifeless food, it makes sense you will be devitalized and lifeless. Your body has nothing on which to draw to keep it energetic and vibrant. If you do not feel like cooking, then eat apples or other fruits or vegetables, sliced or whole. Even though you may crave sugar and junk food, these foods not only do not help in relieving depression, they make it worse. Buy and eat organic foods, if possible. It has not been determined how chemically treated and genetically altered foods affect us, so best to avoid them.

2. Know that you are not insane.

Depression is a warning sign that something is wrong. It is a symptom that something is out of balance in your body, in your environment, or both. We live in an environment filled with toxins. There are wars, inequitable laws, financial pressures, and media overload. The list is unending.

We are natural beings living in an unnatural world. This is the insanity. Our bodies, our minds, and our spirits are reacting to this insanity. Know that you are not insane. You are reacting to the insanity outside you.

3.   Turn the TV off.

Take a break from media overload. Turn the TV off and do not read the newspapers. Most of what you hear on TV and read in the papers is not good news. This is not the time to read and listen to sad stories and ponder devastating events you can do nothing about.

4.   Fake it till you make it.

Sometimes you need to work from the outside in. Act as if you are *not* depressed. How would you walk, talk or sit if you were not depressed? What would you do if you were not depressed? If Publisher's Clearing House came to your door right now with a $5 million check, would you tell them to go away because you are too depressed? Fake it till you make it. Your brain does not know the difference between what is real and what is imagined. Imagine you are *not* depressed.

5.   Dress up.

Wear your good clothes. Do what you can to make yourself look and feel attractive.

6.   Count your blessings.

When you are depressed, sad and perhaps angry, being grateful is not the first thought that comes to your mind. However, this is the perfect time to count your blessings. This is the perfect time to remember there are people who would gladly trade places with you. We have so many things to be thankful for; however, we often take them for granted. With an attitude of gratitude, depression cannot thrive.

7.   Drink water.

You can survive many weeks without food, but only a few days without water. Dehydration will cause your body and your brain to shut down. Being happy and having a great attitude is impossible if your body is dehydrated. Drink plenty of water. One rule is to drink half your body weight in ounces each day. That is, if you weight 200 pounds, drink 100 ounces of water. Drink filtered or spring water if possible. The tap water in many of our cities contains chemicals and, again, we cannot be sure how these chemicals are affecting us.

8.   Listen to motivational tapes.

Do not leave your mind alone to do its "own thing". Obviously, *your* self-talk is not serving you well at this time. Therefore, this is the perfect time to listen to someone else's talk. Listen to motivational and inspirational tapes and music. Bombard your brain with uplifting thoughts from others. If you feel like reading, read uplifting and inspiring material.

9.   Dance.

The body needs to move. Get that blood flowing through your body and your brain! Your brain needs a good supply of blood in order to work properly. But when you are feeling depressed, the idea of exercising is not appealing.

So, dance! Play uplifting and happy music. Play music that reminds you of happy times. Stretch out those parts of your body you are able to stretch. Move, move, move. Dance, dance, dance. Your body, your mind, and your soul will thank you.

10. Remember who you are.

You are a precious entity in this great cosmic Universe. You are a representation of God. There is nothing true of the greatest among us that is not true of you. You are magnificent. Sometimes we forget how wonderful we are. Have you?

Summertime

We'd all pack up my granddad's car,

Felt like we were going far,

Goldsboro's not so far away,

But it seemed like we would ride all day.

My grandma and Aunt Thelma too,

Lived right near Scott's barbecue.

They had some chickens and a dog named spot

And a real pecan tree on their lot.

In the summertime,

In the summertime,

That's what we did,

That's how we lived in the summertime.

In the summertime,

In the summertime,

That's what we did,

That's how we lived in the summertime
When we were kids.

We played all day in the summer sun,
Tag and jacks—boy we had fun.
Hopscotch, house, and hide an' seek,
Jump rope—we could skip all week.

We'd run and play until we dropped.
Red Kool-Aid sure hit the spot.
We made them turn the sprinklers on,
And then we'd all jump in the pond.

In the summertime,
In the summertime,
That's what we did,
That's how we lived in the summertime.
In the summertime,
In the summertime,
That's what we did,
That's how we lived in the summertime
When we were kids.

We had fresh corn and black-eyed peas,
Grandma said, "Eat as much as you please".

She'd get a fresh chicken from her yard,
And fry it all up in a ton of lard.

Grandma kept candy near her chair,
If we looked real sad, then she would share.
The best thing came at the end of the day,
I'd crawl in grandma's bed and float away.

In the summertime,
In the summertime,
That's what we did,
That's how we lived in the summertime.
In the summertime,
In the summertime,
That's what we did,
That's how we lived in the summertime
When we were kids.

When we were kids,
When we were kids.

We all scream for ice cream!

Not Feeling What I Need To Feel

Although I admire you, I can't use you.
I don't want to lead you on and confuse you.
Honesty is important to me,
That's why I'm setting you free,

I'm just not feeling what I need to feel.

You are sensitive and you are handsome,
When you smile, you actually glow.

You are affectionate and intelligent,
My friends say I'm crazy to let you go.

Although I admire you, I can't use you.
I don't want to lead you on and confuse you.
Honesty is important to me,
That's why I'm setting you free,

I'm just not feeling what I need to feel.

You caress my hand as we stroll through the
park,
But darling, I don't feel that romantic spark.

You invest your money well—and that's a good
thing.
But I can't accept this precious engagement
ring.

Although I admire you, I can't use you.
I don't want to lead you on and confuse you.
Honesty is important to me,
That's why I'm setting you free,

I'm just not feeling what I need to feel.

If **everybody** got better, who would there be to be better than?

Remembering Two Septembers

September - (1965):

It was a clear day in the month of September,
A day I shall always remember.
For many nights it replayed itself in my
dreams.
As I asked myself,
What manner of men would go to such
extremes?

Fire trucks from everywhere were on the scene,
Hundreds of policemen looking angry and
mean,
There were huge dogs being held at bay,
Dogs that had been trained for just such a day.

The crowd was orderly-—all we wanted was peace,
And for the prejudice ways of society to cease.

But the fire trucks, the police and the dogs were called for,
To silence us for good and keep us coming in the back door,

To ensure that we remained in our place as second-class,
They readily attacked us with water, dogs and tear gas.

They hooked up those fire-hoses and turned them on.
Their sense of justice had vanished and gone.

The mayor made a speech and said, "I'm taking a firm stand,
Segregation will forever be the law of the land."

When the crowd shouted, "We shall overcome!"
The policemen charged the crowd and yelled racial slurs at some.

They hosed us down with water in the street,
And the police beat some of us and knocked us
off our feet.

Men and women were hurting but they ignored
our screams.
What manner of men would go to such
extremes?

September - (2001):

It was a clear day in the month of September,
A day I shall always remember.
For many nights it replayed itself in my
dreams.
As I asked myself,
What manner of men would go to such
extremes?

Fire trucks from everywhere had rushed to the
scene,
Hundreds of policemen looking anxious—but
not mean.

There were huge dogs being held at bay,
Dogs that had been trained for just such a day.

The crowd was orderly—all they wanted was
peace,
And for the evil ways of this world to cease.

But the fire trucks, the police and the dogs
were called for,
To try to save people who'd been trapped on a
top floor.

The firemen and the police put their lives in
danger,
Many lost their lives while saving a stranger.

When the crowd shouted, "We shall overcome!"
I saw a policeman hugging someone.

I saw some firemen and policemen cry,
"Why did so many people have to die?"

I saw them digging with their bare hands
through the rubble.

Retired officers came back to help in this time of trouble.

They worked through the night and the chill of the rain,
Hoping to ease at least one family's pain.

They worked through the long cold days and nights listening for muted screams,
What manner of men would go to such extremes?

A Note from Racial

Dear Y'all,

"I am old. I am tired. I am ugly. But you will not let me die. Do you think y'all will be 'overcoming' anytime soon?"

Yours truly,

Racial Injustice

Fear Be Gone

I recently received an email that prompted me to answer a poll about what I feared most. I didn't reply to the email because my biggest fear at that moment was the fear of receiving more unsolicited email. However, I did start thinking about the subject of fear. What are we afraid of? What is fear? What can we do about it? We all have fears at one time or another and to one degree or another. I did a little research of my own and found that next to terrorist, fear of public speaking and fear of success ranked high on the list of things people fear most.

Fear of Public Speaking

According to one survey I read, many people fear public speaking more than death. Although most people are not aware of why they have a fear of public speaking on a conscious level, psychological studies have determined that nearly everyone who has a fear of public speaking experienced some major or minor trauma when they were younger that causes them to be fearful of public speaking as teenagers or adults.

Fear of Success

Another high ranking and common fear is fear of success. Success means achieving or accomplishing a goal. Success can mean the attainment of wealth, fame, power or whatever you truly desire for yourself. Success is a good thing. Why, then, are so many of us afraid of success either consciously or unconsciously? It is all about how we perceive success.

Instead of focusing on how good it will feel to finally accomplish our goals, we are focused on the negative aspects. Perhaps we have a memory of a successful person who was ridiculed for having "too much money". Perhaps we remember hearing that it is easier for a poor man to get into the kingdom of heaven or that successful people feel they are better than others. Therefore, we become fearful of what others may say and think about us if we become successful. We often sabotage our own success.

We are not afraid of success itself. We are afraid of what we imagine success might bring with it. We think we might or should feel guilty for having "the good life". We fear making our friends jealous and think they will no longer like us. We fear we are going to have to work harder to maintain our new status. We fear that we'll have to pay huge taxes. We fear that people will try to steal from us. We wonder what would happen if we were to lose our fortune.

A Powerful Emotion

Fear is an emotion and the symptoms of this emotion manifest in each of us in various ways. Some of the symptoms of fear are shallow breathing, sweaty palms, upset stomach, nervousness, headache, inability to speak, inability to think clearly, depression, uncontrollable shaking, inability to moved, and anger. People literally lose their lives and have been known to take someone else's life out of fear. All of the "isms" are the children of fear—racism, chauvinism, classism, and sexism. Wars and crime thrive on fear.

Fear takes away our creativity, imagination, freedom and peace. Fear stops us from pursuing our dreams. Fear destroys relationships and can make us physically ill. These four letters, F E A R, represent the most powerful negative emotion that exists.

And just think, we have all this unhappiness and suffering over something that does not even exist except for the meaning or perception that we give to a person, place, thing or event. Our fears only live because each of us gives our own fears life. The fears we have exist because we nurture them, feed them, and acknowledge them.

Our Past Stories and Imaginations

In other words, our fears are based on our individual perceptions, and our perceptions are based on our individual stories or histories and our imaginations.

How else can we explain the fact that each of us has different fears and fears to different degrees? For instance, there are many people who love dogs. However, there are also people who fear dogs. Some love snakes and have them as pets. Yet, many others are extremely afraid of snakes and become traumatized at the mere sight of them.

Most of the time, we are not even aware of the stories that our fears are based on. Some of us have anxiety attacks and are fearful over a comment that another child made to us when we were small. In other words, we let a child from our past control our life and health today.

Release the Fear

In order to release the fear, we must change our perceptions about a person, event or object. Choose to see it for what it is - a person, an event or an object. Many of us fear things that have not happened and may never happen. We cannot enjoy our lives today because we are fearful of what the future may hold. We can choose to release ourselves from the hold that our past stories and our imaginations have on us.

If you are totally immobilized by fear of something, you can always seek assistance from techniques such as Emotional Freedom Techniques (EFT), Neuro Linguistic Programming (NLP), or hypnotherapy. I encourage you to explore the options each of these techniques provide. Each of them, using their own methods, de-traumatizes past traumas and identify and integrate conflicting belief systems that keep us from doing things we want to do.

In my experience, these types of procedures can bring about relief from fears quickly. Instead of treating the symptoms, as medications do, these techniques and other similar procedures address the cause of the fear.

A Signal for Change

The positive aspect of fear is that it is a signal for change. If someone were to point a gun at us, in the mist of fear, we would hope that something would change for the better. Hopefully, we would think of some way to change the situation without being harmed. When faced with the fear of the possibility of a child being harmed, parents have found physical strength and mental courage that they did not know was possible.

And so it is with our everyday fears. Let fear be a signal to change or move in a new direction. Move beyond your comfort zone. Perhaps we need more knowledge about the person, place, or thing that is causing us to feel fearful. Most importantly, move toward love. Love yourself. Love everyone and everything. Love is the most powerful emotion. Where there is real love, fear will perish.

We Are More Powerful than Fear

In my opinion, failure to remember who we are in relation to God and this great Universe is the number one cause of fear. Where there is no faith, there is fear. The absence of belief in ourselves and what we are capable of creates doubt and fear.

Yes, there will be tragedies. No, things will not always go as you planned. Yes, there will be people who want to say negative things about you. These people would rather comment on what appear to be your flaws rather than deal with their own. Do not give them your power.

None of us are ordinary human beings. All of us are extraordinary divine beings. Everyone has the power that will not fail, should it be acknowledged and embraced. Sometimes, I have to remind myself of this. I say, "Fear, be gone. You have no power here." Just by saying these words, it is as if I turn on a light and I see fear for what it really is—nothing.

You're a Stranger to Me

You don't come 'round no more like you used
to.
And I really, really, really, really need you.

I wish you'd come by for just an hour or so,
Then, if I had to, I'd surely let you go.

It's been such a long time since you were here,
The thought of never seeing you again fills me
with fear.

My nights and days are filled with pain.
Constantly I'm calling out your name.
I say, "Sleep. Sweet, sweet sleep,
You're a stranger to me".

I know you got so many other gals you got to
see.
Maybe you just can't find no time for little ol'
me.

Please, please, don't, don't do me this way.
Come on back here, I need you to stay.

I try not to worry—say everything will be all
right.
But it really makes me crazy when you stay
gone night after night.

My nights and days are filled with pain.
Constantly I'm calling out your name.
I say, "Sleep. Sweet, sweet sleep,
You're a stranger to me".

Sleep, take away the pain.
If you come back here sleep,
Don't ever leave again.

Sleep, sweet sleep, can you mend a broken
soul?
If I ever get you back here sleep,

I refuse to ever let you go!

I tried counting sheep.
But my little woolly friends just ran away from me.
The doctor downtown said, "These pills should help one sleep."
But, as you can see, these pills have had no affect whatsoever on me.
I don't feel like reading nobody's book.
So, I just sit here on my sofa and look.

I sit here all alone.
This house sho' ain't a home.

My head is full of thoughts,
I need to turn them off!

But, sleep just won't come.
Should I dial 9-1-1?

And say, "Sleep. Sweet, sweet sleep is a stranger to me!"

Everyday Nourishment

Did you feed your BODY?

Did you feed your MIND?

Food for Thought

Food
For
Thought

Did you feed your SPIRIT?

Toddlers Eat Vegetables

INTERVIEWER:

So, how do you get your toddlers to eat vegetables?

ME:

I throw the vegetables on the floor and say, "Don't touch that!"

I Who Have No Electric Dishwasher

Washing dishes?
A waste of time, I say.
I wish I could just throw all the dirty dishes
away.

Washing dishes is not my thing.
Although what I eat from I want to be clean.

I didn't write down washing dishes as one of
my 'dream life' plans.
And the worst part about it is not the washing,
but scrubbing those doggone pans.

I tried eating from paper plates
But the food didn't taste too good.
My meals tasted like cheap TV dinners,
Nothing tasted like it should.

Once I tried throwing the dirty dishes away,
But buying new dishes all the time took all my
pay.

I tried eating all of my meals out at places I
could afford,
But after a week I gave that up,
With McDonald's I got too bored.

I tried not eating anything at all—
That way my dishes would stay clean.
All I got was hungry and tired—
Not to mention irritable and mean.

I think I'll have a lady come in just once a week
or so,
Just to wash the dishes (and maybe mop the
floor).

I'm just gonna have to hire me a maid to come
in every now and then,
'Cause I'll be damned if I'm gonna keep wash-
ing these dishes over and over again.

Sweet Kiss, Hot Sex

Sweet kiss
Hot sex

The evening went quite well.
Now I'm waking it up in fancy five-star hotel.

The service was fabulous in every way.
Then he says, "There is something I forgot to say".

He says he has a family.

"My girls are dynamite.
But that wife of mine just loves to fuss and fight.
I wish that she too
Could understand me like you do".

I'm not a fool,
Somehow I knew.
But last night I had nothing better to do.

Sweet kiss
Hot sex

He says, "I'll give you a call when I come back
in town,
I hope you'll be able to come back around".

Sweet kiss
Hot sex

9 Steps toward Nontoxic Health and Beauty

1.   Make your own deodorant.

You can make your own deodorant by adding together equal parts of baking soda and cornstarch. This is a wonderful recipe for deodorant, and it works. The baking soda absorbs the odor. The cornstarch absorbs the wetness.

2.   Perfumes are not necessarily your friend.

Perfumes can be costly and may contain toxins. Pure essential oils can keep you smelling heavenly. Essential oils have also been proven to have many healing benefits.

3.   Read the label.

Sometimes it is as simple as reading the label. Though many labels are purposely misleading, reading the label will help us know whether a product is one that we want to put in or on our bodies. If you see a long list of ingredients, and you don't know what most of them are or what they do, you probably want to avoid that product.

4.   Check your kitchen.

The best products for our beauty and health are often in our kitchens. Nature provides wonderful fruits, vegetable, seeds and berries, many of which make the best cosmetics and body-care products. Somehow or other, we have learned to doubt Nature. We feel that we know best. We have gone against the laws of Nature in favor of commercialism.

5.   Wash new clothes before you wear them.

The clothes you buy go through many processes and many hands before you buy them yourself. If the garment is washable, please be sure to wash it before you wear it for the first time. This will ensure that excess chemicals, pesticides, dyes and bleaches are removed before it meets your body.

6.   Our body is one unit.

We often forget that our body is one unit. Many of us have the idea that it is all right to use toxic products on our hair, for instance. We believe that a product used outside our body will not affect the inside of our body. This is not true. Therefore, If you would not put a product in your body (eat it), please do not put it on your body. The reverse holds true.

7.   Less is more.

Many of us have cabinets full of cosmetics and so-called health products. We are bombarded constantly with products that promise to make us healthy, youthful and beautiful. However, the truth is, less is more. Find products with the least amount of ingredients. Single ingredient products, such as coconut oil, Shea butter or various clays, are superb products. Likewise, an occasional meal that consists only of one nutritious food will give your digestive system a rest.

8.   Research.

We spend a great deal of time researching vacation spots we want to travel to. We will ask in-depth questions about whether the car we're thinking of buying gets good mileage and drives well. However, we spend little time researching the products that we put in and on our bodies. Our bodies are our temples. Learn about your body and the food and products you consume.

9.   Talk to your elders.

Many of our ancestors knew the health and beauty secrets of the plants and the earth. Over the years, however, we have been taught to discount their knowledge of health and beauty as old-fashioned. The beauty and health industry would love you to believe this. Do not let our elders take these secrets with them to the grave.

Before I Let Go and Let God

Let go and let God is the advice
My minister gave to me.
He said whenever I feel disturbed, just be still
and let things be.

He said I don't have to carry any burden all on
my own;
That if I let go and if I let God,
A miraculous way will be shown.

I'm going to let go and I'm going to let God.
I believe what my minister says is true.
However, because my boss is so mean to me,
there are a few other things I have to do too.

I'm going to beat my boss in his big head with
this steel office chair.

I'll pour gasoline on his scalp before I pull out
each strand of his hair.

I will pull his tiny eyeballs out with my two
bare hands,
And dice up his nasty, lying tongue
And put the pieces in the trash cans.

I shall squash his fingers and bash up his toes,
While squeezing his heart until no blood flows.

I'll fling a sharp object into his hairy back,
And hang his fatty ribs from a butchers meat
rack.

And after I twist both of his legs around this
hot iron rod
And stomp on him with football cleats till he's
as limp as broiled cod;

Then, I'm going to sit down at my office desk
and have myself some lunch.
I'm going to have a Caesar salad and a bottle of
raspberry punch.

Then, I'm going to play a little Marvin Gaye on
my new iPod.
Then, close my eyes—inhale—exhale
Now, I *let go and let God.*

Right Back (Where I Started From)

Everything looks so familiar to me.
I've been at this place before.
I really thought I was going somewhere,
But I'm right back at the very same door.

I used to think I was going far.
Even dreamed about being a star
And even though I had myself a pretty good
run,
I'm right back, right back, right back where I
started from—where I started from.

If you should ever see my friends,
Please don't tell them that you saw me here.
I was supposed to be somebody,
Now I just want to disappear.

I did everything they told me to,
I treated people kind and I stayed in school.

But Instead of being the star of some smash hit
sitcom,
I'm right back, right back, right back where I
started from—where I started from.

I don't understand myself
What has happened to me.
I told myself a thousand times
This ain't how it's supposed to be.

I should be moving on.
But here I stand—everything's going wrong.

Out here on my own,
Facing the unknown,
Feeling all alone,
All my dreams are gone.

Going right back—going right on back home.

It kind of hurts me when they talk about me
With no compassion in their hearts.

Many say I'm just acting a fool,
But I really don't want to play this part.

That's why I close my windows and doors.
I can't hang with the crowd no more.

Living like I'm living just ain't no fun.
I'm right back, right back, right back, right
back, right back, right back, right back, right
back, right back

Where I started from,
Where I started from.

Yes, the Truth Shall Set You Free

"The greatest obstacle to discovery is not ignorance - it is the illusion of knowledge." - Daniel J. Boorstin

Get inspired to seek the truth! Let's be inspired to think differently. Get motivated to move away from the pack and celebrate your uniqueness. Step back and look at yourself, the world and everything with a different perspective—your perspective.

When we think about the things we do each day and the way we do them, we find there is no valid reason for doing some of them. We do them because everybody else does and because it has "always been done that way". Or, because it can feel uncomfortable being different.

Many of us live our lives on autopilot. Life is hectic; therefore, we find it convenient to accept what the newspaper says, the politician says, or even what our neighbors and relatives say is true as fact. I encourage you to seek your own truth. Think for yourself.

Many facts are stranger than fiction. Be aware of what is going on around you. Ask questions. Do not just follow the leader. Think for yourself. Look at both sides of a story and then follow your instinct.

If someone says that you do not need to see a certain movie or read a certain book or listen to a certain person because of his or her point of view, you had better believe that is the exact movie, book or person you want to investigate for yourself.

What a man says and what is are two different things. Be careful to whom you give your trust. No man or woman has any power that is greater than your power. The government or the powers-that-be cannot save you. Only you can save you. Hold on to your power and trust yourself. Get the facts. Know the truth.

"One of the first means or measures to which the slave-holder resorts in subjecting the slave to his control, is to destroy his thinking powers." - Frederick Douglass

A Slave Xmas Tale

'Twas the night before Christmas, and all through the plantation, the slave master said to his slaves, "No picking cotton this week.
It's time for your yearly reward.
This week we celebrate the birth of our Lord."

"See what we do for you slaves.
No backbreaking fieldwork for seven whole days."

"Now listen up and I'll tell you what I'm gonna do;
I'm gonna kill one of my biggest hogs and share my pork with you."

"Go have yourselves a jolly old Christmastime!
I don't want to use my whip for any reason,

And I won't have to if you behave yourselves
during this holiday season."

$$$$$

Now, there were those slaves who used this
time to finally do something for self.
They made corn brooms, mats, baskets, and
quilts from scraps of fabric that were left.

Some hunted or made carvings of wood,
Or helped another slave if they could.

The master frowned upon these slaves—the
ones who made 'the most' of each day—

The ones who used the time to get to know one
another,
Reflect on their strengths, or honor an elderly
mother.

These were the slaves that made the master
uneasy.
The master would be nervous all day.

He hated to see his slaves thinking and plan-
ning.
What if they figured out how to get away?

$$$$

Now the other group of slaves, who outnum-
bered the rest,
Were the slaves the master really liked best.

They spent their time getting drunk as could
be.
The master didn't share many things,
But at Christmastime, he was more than happy
to give his slaves some whisky.

Master loved the good ol' slaves who drank a lot
of gin.
They'd stumble and fall and wallow in the pig-
pen.

Master would say, "Man, these slaves sho'
know how to celebrate.
I love to see 'em like this—happy and drunk
and playing a little sport—

Come on, drink up y'all. Here's another quart."

"I like these good ol' slaves and I'm glad they're
my own.
Just look at em' drinking' and partying' and
carrying' on.
When I see 'em like this, I know I can sleep,
They're just wandering around like little lost
sheep."

Master would laugh so hard his belly would
shake like a bowl full of jelly.

"This Christmastime thing is all right with me.
Them good ol' slaves party so hard, they forget
that they ain't free.
They forget that they belong to me!
Ho! Ho! Ho!"

$$$$$

Such was Christmas on the old plantation
wa-a-a-ay back then;
And it is still pretty much business as usual
here in 2010.

We wait for the master to tell us when

We should buy presents for family or friends.

Even then, we are not filled with cheer

Until he tells us which gifts are 'in' each year.

Little Ieesha wanted that doll way back in July,

But, you told her to wait and that if she was good,

The fat white man would bring it by and by.

With the Master *in* charge, we can buy a lot of presents with Visa, Discover or American Express.

Our kids do deserve the very best.

However, after we use up all our credit, we do not take credit for the good we've done.
We tell our children that Santa brought it—that *he* is the special one.

Master will still give you a fancy bottle filled with whisky,
And perhaps invite you to his Christmas party.

Master is so lively and quick. Master will laugh and say,
"I can't discuss that promotion or raise, get back to me after the holidays."

The tinsel, the stockings, the ribbons, the bow,
The holly, the chitlins, the lights and mistletoe;

The shopping, the cards, the traffic, the tree,
"I'm not getting her a present. What did she get me?"

Is this really what we want to do?
I'm just saying that maybe it's time to really
think this Christmas thing through.

Some of us say, "We just want to celebrate the
birth of Jesus."
Jesus, we will always remember.
However, any honest historian will tell you
baby Jesus was not born in December.

"It's tradition," you say.
"My family has always done it this way."

I don't mean to fuss, but we need to make sure
that this Christmas thing is something that
benefits us.
When I was a child, it was tradition to ride In
the back of the bus.

$$\$\$\$\$$$

And, I heard Master exclaim as he drove out of
sight,
"This Christmastime thing is really all right!"

"I was worried when I heard the slaves were free,
And that I would have to pay them for working for me."

"But, now I know that law don't mean 'jack,'
'cause I pay 'em all year long, but at
Christmastime
They give all the money right back!
Ho! Ho! Ho!"

$$$$$ $$$$$ $$$$$ $$$$

========================

"So, when the holidays ended, we staggered up from the filth of our wallowing, took a long breath, and marched to the field,—feeling, upon the whole, rather glad to go, from what our master had deceived us into a belief was freedom, back to the arms of slavery." – *Frederick Douglass, Narrative of the Life of Frederick Douglass, an American Slave*

Keep Self-love Alive

Having a loving relationship with you is extremely important. Unlike relationships with other people, you cannot leave yourself. Wherever you go, you are going with you. Therefore, the relationship you have with yourself must be nurtured. Honestly and deeply loving yourself is necessary for you to honestly and deeply and healthily love another.

If you think divorcing someone else is stressful, painful and financially devastating, try divorcing yourself. Ouch! Not pretty. You cannot leave yourself.

Therefore, learn to LOVE YOUR WONDERFUL, POWERFUL, MAGNIFICENT SELF!

On the following page are . . .

5 Things You Can Do
To Help Keep Your Self-love Alive

☼ **1. Learn to say, "I love me"—and mean it. "Fake it till you make it."**

I've met many people who cannot say they love themselves. Some think that it is almost sacrilegious to say, "I love me." If you can't say it and mean it, then I suggest you fake it until you make it. *Act* as if you love you. The psyche doesn't know the difference between what is real and what is imagined. Before long, you will start to believe it—and feel it. Trust me; you're going to feel real good when you admit that you love you.

☼ **2. Forgive yourself.**

Some people feel they are undeserving of self-love because of mistakes or 'bad' things they've done in the past. Whatever we may have done or said or did not do or did not say, you are forgiven. If you believe that you have to wait for God to forgive you, know that you have already been forgiven. God is not a vengeful God. God / the Universe wants you to be happy. Also, you can and do have the power to forgive yourself.

Learn from your mistakes. If possible, apologize and do what you can to make things right and move on to higher ground. Don't spend your life suffering.

☼ **3. Honor yourself.**

Yes. You deserved to be honored. You are a child of God / the Universe. Do you think God would create something that was not worth honoring? Honor yourself by feeding your mind, body and spirit the best that the Universe has to offer. Would you put something called 'junk gas' in your car? Then, why would you put something called 'junk food' in your body? Respect yourself. Honor yourself.

Don't stay in relationships or environments that do not serve you well.

☼ **4. Take yourself on a date.**

When two people are attracted to each other, they want to spend time alone. Couples go out on dates to get to know each other better.

Every now and then, spend some time alone with just *you*. Take *yourself* on dates. Use the time alone to take inventory of your life and make decisions on what new directions and adventures you'd like to explore. Reconnect with your inner strength and wisdom. Play music, read, take yourself to a concert or play or treat yourself to a delicious meal.

However, don't be afraid of silence —or afraid of what you might find out about *you*.

☼ 5. Don't take yourself too seriously.

Find the humor in some of the things that you do and say. Find humor in your world and your environment. Laugh, dance, sing. Find hobbies that interest you and bring out your joy. Don't be afraid to let your "inner child" out and play.

Think

In the summer of 1968, I remember dancing and singing along with Aretha Franklin as she wailed, "You better think! Yeah, Think! Let your mind go. Let yourself be free!"

Whether I was washing the dishes, doing homework, or just hanging out with my friends, whenever I heard that song, I'd stop whatever I was doing and belt out at least one, "Think!" myself. Of course, I also owned the 45 record. I loved that song. For three weeks, *Think* was the number one R&B single in the United States.

During that same summer, I was preparing to go away to college. I had taken the right test and had gotten the right scores, so surely I knew how to think. Yes, I knew how to think. I have come to realize, over the years, that while I knew *how* to think, I didn't understand the power of thinking or the power of thoughts.

While I celebrated *Think* being the number one R&B single, I failed to realize that thinking was then, is now, and forever and always will be the number one factor in what determines the quality of our lives. "Yeah, you better think."

I didn't realize that I was creating what I was thinking about. Because of this, I created some real messes. Oh, don't get me wrong; I created some wonderful adventures too. For the most part, however, I was busy thinking as a reaction to what was going on around me. I was thinking on automatic.

I was not totally in charge of my thinking. Therefore, I was not totally in charge of my life. I was imaginative and very creative in all areas that pertained to the arts—theater, crafts, and writing. However, it never occurred to me to apply that same imagination and creativity to every aspect of my life.

Psychological studies show that each of us has about 60,000 thoughts each day. That's a lot of thoughts. Yes, that's the good news. Here's the sad news. We are not having 60,000 new thoughts each day. Most of us are thinking the same few little thoughts over and over again 60,000 times. ("My boss is getting on my nerves." My boss really gets on my nerves." "I got to find me a new job." "I'm going to quit this job." "I'm going to quit this job because my boss gets on my nerves." "Did I tell you what my boss did?" "He acts like I'm stupid." "He really made me angry." "My boss . . .")

I now realize that just like I didn't understand the power of my thoughts, most other people do not realize how powerful their thoughts are either. Most of us do not realize that the Universe, or God, or whatever we call the greatest power is busy creating for us what we think and create in our minds. Our thoughts are powerful things. They are energy. Our thoughts carry vibration messages throughout the Universe. They bring to us more of whatever we are thinking about.

Therefore, if we are concentrating and thinking about how bad things are, we are creating more bad things. If we constantly think about things that really don't matter, we create more stuff in our lives that doesn't matter. Knowing who was voted out of the house on a reality TV show really is not going to affect our lives unless we are that person who was voted off or we are somehow personally connected to that person.

We spend time thinking about and discussing movie characters, how to beat electronic games, discuss other people's business, and what's wrong or right about our political system. True, we are not hurting anybody and yes, there are worse things we could be doing. However, we are not really helping ourselves either. We can use the time that we spend thinking about things that don't really matter to us to create completely new lives for ourselves.

Imagine if we spent this time thinking and planning our own lives—thinking about ways to make our own lives better and thinking about things that we want to have, to be, and to do. Think about what *is* right in our lives. We're not taking advantage of the simple, yet, remarkable gift that each of us has been given—the power to think. It doesn't cost us one cent to think. Learn to appreciate the magic of thinking and being able to *choose* what we think about.

Aretha sang to her man, "Think about what you trying to do to me". I challenge *you* to think about what you're trying to do to *yourself.* You have the power to think yourself into a place of joy, a place of peace and yes, even a place of health and wealth. Think about it.

If It Weren't for that Damn War

I run out in my yard,
Tell everybody I see,
"I don't know who they are,
But, there are some colored people on TV".

I pick up the telephone and
Call everybody I know,
I say, "Tonight, The Supremes are going to be
on the Ed Sullivan show".

*****

And what about those white boys with hair so
long you can hardly see an ear.
They traveled all the way from England to sing
their songs over here.
I love you yeah, yeah, yeah—that's one of the
songs they sing in their show.

Let's see, John, Paul, George—and they called
the drummer Ringo.

*****

Ruthie said next month there's going to be a
Motown Review.
She said besides Stevie Wonder, Ike and Tina
Turner might be there too.
I sure do hope my mama lets me go,
I'd hate to miss a terrific R&B soul show.

*****

I never miss an episode of Soul Train.
No matter what—cold, flu or stomach pain,
That's how I always know the latest dance
moves.
Man, how I love watching those beautiful
colored people groove.

*****

Billy Stewart sang, *Sitting in the park* . . .
The Young Rascals sang, *Groovin' on a Sunday
afternoon* . . .
Aretha Franklin sang, *Daydreaming and I'm
thinking of you* . . .
Dionne Warwick sang, *If you see me walking
down the street* . . .

Little Anthony sang, *I know you don't know what I'm going through standing here looking at you . . .*

Brenda Holloway sang, *Every little bit hurts . . .*

The Five Stairsteps sang, *Ooh-o-o child things are gonna get easier . . .*

James Brown sang, *Say it loud (I'm Black and I'm proud) . . .*

****

I danced with my friends.

Yes, we had some great fun.

But sometimes I wonder how much more we could have done,

If it weren't for that damn war.

That damn

Vietnam

War

The Universal Menu

We order from the Universal Menu every second of every day. (We make selections from all that is available to us In the Universe.) Most of us are not aware that we are ordering with each thought we think. However, that is how we end up with so many things on 'our life plate' that we would like to send back.

Many of us live day to day on automatic. That is, we forget that we have the power to choose not only our thoughts, but, also our emotions. Our thoughts and emotions feed our subconscious mind and send a signal to the Universe. The Universe responds by turning our thoughts and emotions into our 'things'—our environment—our situations—our lives.

The subconscious mind / God / the Universe are busy 24/7 manufacturing whatever it thinks we want. Whatever we are thinking about or focused on or feeling; the Universe assumes that is what we want and creates that for us. The subconscious mind has no sense of humor, takes literally every word, thought, emotion and deed we experience, and creates more of the same — whether good or bad. That's a Universal law.

We spend a great portion of our lives reacting to events and situations instead of being proactive and creating the lives that we desire and deserve. Focus on what you do want and you'll get that. Focus on what you do not want and you'll get that.

The thoughts we have when we wake up and our first activities in the morning set the tone for the rest of our day (and many times our lives).

From the moment we wake up, before we even get out of bed, we need to consciously choose what type of day we want to have and how we want to feel, and then claim it.

Release your desires to the Universe.

My Universal Menu allows you to focus on what it is you do want to create for yourself. With our hectic lifestyles, we don't always create the time to decide deliberately and on purpose what we do desire to have and feel each day. However, not doing this is exactly why (for some of us)—we have days where we keep asking ourselves, "Why do I have so many problems?" or "Why is everything so difficult?"

The Universe is here to serve you. You are here to serve the Universe.

Now, for what I believe is the best news ever!

The best way to serve and honor the Universe, is to serve and honor *Yourself*.

It doesn't get much better than that.

Allow yourself to be served.

Do not worry about how all of the wonderful dreams and ideas you desire and focus on will come true. The Universe is great at figuring out that kind of stuff. All you have to do is keep focusing on and ordering all that is good for you.

<u>Choose what you want to have.</u>

Place your order now.

I invite you to have a look at the

Universal Menu on the next page.

I believe you will find some choices that you simply cannot live without.

The Universe is here to serve you.

It will serve you whatever you choose.

Please choose carefully.

Each day make a conscious choice of what you would like to be served.

You will be served something today whether you choose or not.

You have a choice.

Each day put a check to the left of your choices.

Universal Menu

joy	health	peace
energy	love	pity
fear	pride	knowledge
laughter	hopelessness	sorrow
anxiety	confidence	wealth
overwhelm	forgiveness	hate
faith	grief	excuses
guilt	pain	fun
freedom	success	enthusiasm
sadness	beauty	struggle
wisdom	happiness	courage

Write in three side dishes.

Sample: "I will eat healthy today" or

"I will take the action necessary to find a better place to live"

Side dish 1:

Side dish 2:

Side dish 3:

Tipping is not necessary.

Being Grateful is Mandatory.

I am **A**mazing. I am **B**eautiful. I am **C**ourageous. I am **D**ivine. I am **E**volving. I am **F**antastic. I am **G**orgeous. I am **H**ealthy. I am **In**terested. I am **J**oyful. I am **K**ind. I am **L**ove. I am **M**agnificent. I am **N**otable. I am **O**pen-minded. I am **P**recious. I am **Q**uotable. I am **Re**joicing. I am **S**trong. I am **T**errific. I am **U**nstoppable. I am **V**ictorious. I am **W**ise. I am **X**enialistic*. I am **Y**outhful. I am **Z**estful.

*Hospitable, especially to visiting strangers or foreigners.

Pledge of Allegiance to Myself

We commit and are loyal to many people and many ideas—including our flag and our country. However, do we have the same commitment to ourselves?

Do we love respect and cherish ourselves as we love respect and cherish things outside of us?

Are we loyal enough to ourselves to be mindful of what we allow ourselves to think, eat and allow in our personal space?

This is my pledge—a reminder of my faithfulness to myself. I share this pledge with you. You may make it your own or create your own pledge of allegiance to yourself.

I place my hand over my heart and I say:

I pledge allegiance to myself!

I pledge allegiance to myself and to God whom I personify.

I am indivisible from my wisdom and my magnificence.

I am respecting liberty, encouraging justice, and sharing love.

I am protecting, loving and respecting myself, knowing that there are those who cannot, will not or refuse to protect, love, respect or see me as the beautiful and powerful energy that I AM in this great cosmos.

I do not hate or hold a grudge. However, I defend my right to feel and express my emotions and seek justice using all of my Earthly wisdom and spiritual knowledge, spiritual power and spiritual connections.

I live boldly and will—one day depart this life with dignity.

I pledge allegiance to myself!

New Love

Perhaps he saw the flowers that I kept bringing home.
Or, how lately, I requested a little more time for me to
be alone.

Maybe it was the smile that had become a permanent
fixture on my face.
Or, perhaps he noticed that my lingerie was accented
with a little bit more lace.

Whatever it was he somehow knew that something
was different with me.
Like a fool, I believed that it was my secret—that no
one else could see.

Sometimes I felt uneasy—even a little guilty—perhaps
I should tell,

But I needed more time—I needed to be sure—my secret could wait just as well.

*****

It took me by surprise when I heard him whispering to someone on the telephone.
He said, "I hate to do this but a man has a right to know what's going on".

I heard him when he made the call.
I got real close to the door and heard it all.

He said, "It is obvious there is a new love somewhere,
I don't want to be played like a fool.
Send me your best guys from your most impressive private eye school.
I'll pay you guys two thousand a day."

He hired these 'private eyes' to follow me night and day,
Trying to catch my new love interest and me in some compromising way.

Deceit was not my intention
Lying is not my game.
But a woman's got to do what a woman's got to do,

This woman felt no shame.

I can't hide my emotions—just make them go away.
Love is mighty powerful and I knew this love was here
to stay.

One morning I arose just before dawn and bathed in
warm water with delicate bubbles everywhere.
I dusted myself with fine powder and added a fresh
rose scent to my hair.

When I stepped into my yard that morning,
The sun embraced me with her warmth
But I felt cold eyes watching me.
I felt a presence behind me,
But every time I looked around, no one did I see.

I took a step,
They took a step.
I stopped,
They stopped.

An explosion of flash bulbs when off in my face.
Then, they looked at me and smiled and started the
chase.

Red lights on the video cameras were aglow,
Following me everywhere I would go.

I turned this way,
They turned this way.
If I went right,
They went right.

I ran.
They ran — oh yes, it was on!

I ran down to the lake.
The water was cool and clear.
There were yellow and purple daffodils growing
everywhere.

I skipped over to the meadow,
The grass was green and thick.
The grass beckoned me and I answered,
I took off all my clothes and laid down in it.

The sun kissed me all over.
I felt brand-new.
Yes. I was in love—I had a new love.

Yes, it was true.

I climbed a nearby mountain and I stood on the very edge.
I could have taken any cloud I wanted but I grabbed a rainbow instead.

I wrapped the rainbow around my shoulders—and made a rainbow skirt too,
And then I sprinkled my face with the early morning dew.

Helicopters were circling overhead.
There was nowhere to hide—so I ran some more instead.

A few private eye guys were hanging from a tree,
With cameras posed, ready to expose my new love's identity.

Finally, when I could run no more,
I dropped my knees to the ground.
I shook my head and looked up smiling.
My new love would not let me frown.

I laughed out loud to myself.

"Busted!" I shouted to myself.

I threw my arms in the air and then I embraced myself.

I yelled, "Are y'all blind?"

"Can't you see?"

"My New Love,

My New Love,

My New Love is ME!"

I Forgot

I forgot to be joyful.

I forgot to rejoice.

I forgot—just don't be vexed by this material world.

Don't listen to ignorant men.

I forgot to remember that the answers are within.

I forgot about my power.

I forgot about my strength.

I forgot not to worry 'bout what you see,

'Cause there's a whole lot more to me.

I forgot to remember that the answers are within.

I forgot I was big.

I forgot I was tall.

I forgot not to worry 'bout everybody else's stuff,
My own life is enough.
I forgot to remember that the answers are within.

I forgot. I forgot. I forgot. I forgot.
Couldn't remember.
I forgot. I forgot. Yes. I forgot.
Please forgive me.
I forgot. Yes I forgot.

Now I know about my power.
Now I know about my strength.
I know not to care what people see
'Cause there's a whole lot more to me.
'Cause I know that I know that I know . . .

*****

*And I made a promise to myself : On those days
when I'm not sure that I can continue to hang in
here—or, even why I should—when the chal-
lenges are overwhelming, I will take one day at
a time knowing that before long I will start to
remember what I forgot –*

I forgot about my power . . .

My mama said, "If *they* were going to save us, *they* would have done so already".

My mama used to say, "Action speaks louder than words".

Year after year I hear politicians and corporations say what *they* are going to do. *They* have convinced us that the answer lies with them—in a new law—a new bill—a new committee—a new board—a new focus group—a new plan—a new CEO—a new agency—a new pharmaceutical drug—a new governor or mayor or president.

However, the solution to joyful and healthy lives is within each of us. Each of us is born with all we need to be happy and well. Yet, we are encouraged to look to everyone and everything except ourselves.

They are not going to save us.

About the Author

Wambui Bahati (a.k.a. John Ann Washington) is an entertainer, author and speaker. She began her formal theatrical studies at New York University School of the Arts. Her numerous theater credits include starring roles on Broadway, Broadway show tours, regional and stock theater.

Wambui wrote, produced and stars in the one-woman shows, *Balancing Act – the Musical* (about mental illness) and *I Am Domestic Violence*. Both of these shows have received national acclaim for the unique way that they provide outstanding entertainment while dealing with important issues in our communities.

The native North Carolinian lives in New York City and is the proud mother of two adult daughters. She is the author of the highly acclaimed, tell-all, autobiographical empowerment book, *You Don't Know Crazy—My Life Before, During, After, Above and Beyond Mental Illness* and *Domestic Violence and Relationship Abuse, Awareness and Prevention, for College Women—A Reminder*. Her passion: "Reminding You of Your Magnificence".

Visit: **www.wambui.com** or Call: **888-224-2267.**

Other Books by this Author

Domestic Violence and Relationship Abuse, Awareness and Prevention, for College Women —A Reminder

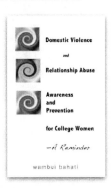

****

You Don't Know Crazy —My Life Before, During, After, Above and Beyond Mental Illness

****

All books are available at all online bookstores. Ask at your favorite 'brick and mortar' bookstore.